"ART, FEAT AND MYSTERY"

The story of Thomas Webb & Sons, Glassmakers

H.W. Woodward

To the craftsmen, past and present, of the Stourbridge Glass Industry.

First published 1978 by Mark + Moody Limited,
Stourbridge, West Midlands DY8 1DQ, England.

ISBN 0 9506439 0 4.

Printed in Great Britain by Mark + Moody Limited,
Stourbridge, West Midlands DY8 1DQ

Preface

1978 seems an appropriate year in which to publish a short history of the firm of Thos. Webb and Sons, Dennis Glass Works, Amblecote, near Stourbridge. One hundred years ago, in 1878, Webb glass achieved its greatest success, the award of the Grand Prix at the Paris Exhibition, with a personal distinction for the head of the firm, Thomas Webb the Second.

Webb's is one of the few glass firms in the Stourbridge district to have survived and progressed for more than a century. Glass making has been an industry in the area, which included the town itself, Amblecote, Wordsley, Kingswinford, Brierley Hill and Dudley, since the early part of the 17th century. In those early days only window glass and bottles were made. During the 18th century "fine flint glass," coloured glass, and drinking glasses with colour twist stems were produced. By the end of the century the art of cutting glass, imported from the Continent and London, was being practised: this was the type of glass for which Stourbridge became especially famous in recent times.

During the 19th century great improvements were made in both glass making and glass decorating, Stourbridge becoming noted for fine decorative and table glass.

Webb's was one of the leading firms in this march of progress, the result of improved knowledge, experiment and skill. The firm's history, therefore, is an important chapter in the story of Stourbridge glass, and indeed, in that of English glass.

A number of people have kindly helped me in the preparation of this work, and to them I offer my sincere and grateful thanks. Mr. S. R. Eveson, the Firm's Technical Director, has generously and tolerantly given me the benefit of his time and expert knowledge. Mr. H. J. Haden, historian of the Stourbridge district and its glass industry, has helped in many valuable ways. Various members of Webb staff have also assisted, especially Mr. E. A. Stott, Managing Director, Mr. F. M. Flockton, and Mr. David Hammond, Chief Designer. By courtesy of Dudley Metropolitan Borough Council items from the Dudley and Brierley Hill Glass Collections are illustrated, Mr. Charles Hajdamach and Mr. Roger Dodsworth of the Museums staff having been particularly helpful. Thanks are also due to Mr. Anthony Waugh for his valuable help; to Birmingham Reference Library and Mr. John Guest, Mark & Moody Ltd., and Sotheby's of London. Also, throughout the time I have been writing this history, and for many years before, I have talked to so many craftsmen in the district that it is impossible to list them all. To these I owe a background knowledge which to me is fascinating as well as being most useful. This little work is therefore dedicated to them and their forebears.

H.W.W.
February 1978

Introduction : Glass through the ages

The nature of glass

More than half the earth's surface consists of silica (silicon dioxide). This mineral is the main ingredient of glass, whether natural or man-made. Nature has created glass in a number of ways, crystallizing silica over millions of years through heat, pressure and moisture to form rock crystal, completely colourless, or the coloured varieties of silica crystals, semi-precious stones, such as amethyst, topaz-citrine, tigereye, chrsysoprase, jasper, chalcedony, cornelian, heliotrope, moss-agate, and agate. The colouration is the result of the presence of minute quantities of metallic oxides, otherwise they are pure silica. Other gem-stones, such as emeralds, contain silica in varying proportions.

But nature has more spectacular ways of glass-making. In volcanic action silica is fused, flows in the lava stream, and when cooled appears as volcanic glass, or obsidian, a blackish glass much used by Stone Age man for implements and weapons. When lightning strikes the desert sand a pillar of glass is formed from the sand it fuses, these natural phenonema are known as fulgurites. More mysterious are tektites, or australites, found in Texas or Australia (and other parts of the world but with different names). In appearance they are like obsidian, and could be silica from the moon fused in flight, or earthly silica fused by meteorites as they strike the earth.

Early glass

All this has a bearing on man-made glass. Throughout the ages man has made glass, using mainly silica and heat, simply adding other ingredients to assist in fusing and to make his product more suitable for its intended purpose. Copying nature, he gives his glasses the same names: "crystal" glass, amethyst, aventurine, ruby, opal, alabaster, agate, when he succeeds. Man-made glass, is, however, not crystalline, but amorphous.

When and where glass was first made is a question which may never be answered completely, but it is almost certain that Mesopotamia is the country which has the distinction of being the home of glass. Some authorities date the earliest glass as far back as 4000 B.C. while others say at least 2700B.C. A Babylonian clay tablet refers to the making of glazes, giving ingredients and the religious rites to be observed; this has been identified as the work, incised about 1670 B.C., of a priest of Marduck. Almost certainly the early metal-workers smelting their copper ores, such as malachite, accidentally fused silica (with the soda and lime also present in their "earths"). This new substance, first used as a glaze, became a substance in its own right, firstly as solid objects such as beads and cartouches, then as vessels formed on a "sand-core." "Sand-core" vessels were made in this manner. A core of clay, and sand, with binding material (even camel dung) was made to the required shape and baked fixed to a tapering metal rod. The core was then revolved in molten glass until it was covered: other parts or decorations were added later. When the vessel was cool, the rod was pulled out and the core scraped out.

About 50 B.C. the Syrians discovered the art of blowing glass: a revolutionary development. From that time vessels could be produced in far greater quantities and blown in moulds for shape or decoration.

No doubt the Egyptians utilised the glass craftsmen of neighbouring countries, in turn so did the Romans. The Syrians certainly have a long tradition in glass, appearing again when Venice revived the art in the 12th century.

In Roman times glass skills reached their zenith in the carving of cameo glass such as the Portland Vase, made during the 1st century B.C./A.D., and in the dietreta cage cups, like the Lycurgus cup of the 4th century A.D. Both these priceless specimens are in the British Museum, London.

With the fall of the Roman Empire and the coming of the Dark Ages, when Europe was over-run by barbarians, only in Persia did art glass-making survive. Here some beautiful gilt and enamel decorated glass-wares, notably mosque lamps, were produced.

Venetian glass

The Renaissance saw many arts and sciences flourish, especially in Italy. Venice and Murano, and Altare in north west Italy, became glass centres. From the 14th century Venetian glass, a soda-lime variety, blown thinly, and at a later date, into fussy and fantastic shapes, relied mainly for effect on shape, colour, applied or painted decoration. Venice became famous for its blue and green glass, its filigree, millefiori, and mosaic glass. It was also noted for its cristallo—the best crystal glass produced so far, although by modern standards it was not nearly colourless, having a brownish tinge. But wherever glass was made in Europe during the 16th and 17th centuries it was made *a la facon de Venise.* Then, beginning in the 18th century, it was ousted by the lime-potash glass of Central Europe and the lead-potash of England. These two types were suitable for cutting and engraving, whereas soda-lime glass, being harder, was not.

Glass in England

Glass had been made in England during Roman times, furnaces having been found in such places as Wilderspool in Lancashire, and on a site near Norwich. But the glass made was mainly window glass. Most Roman glass found in Britain was imported. Many fine cathedrals and churches featured stained glass windows. Bede mentions the glazing of Wearmouth monastery about 675 A.D. by foreign glass-workers. It seems probable that some stained glass, window glass, and vessels, *were* made in Britain.

The Weald of Kent, Surrey, and Sussex, was the scene of glass-making from the 13th century. There was a good supply of green-sand, potash could easily be made from beech wood or bracken, and above all there was then a plentiful supply of timber for firing the furnaces.
Workers from France, where they were regarded as noble, *Les gentilhommes verriers,* and Englishmen, carried on their craft in the Weald, making window glass and bottles. But by the 16th century the quality of their work was not considered good enough. In 1567 Jean Carré, a rather cosmopolitan speculator from Antwerp, obtained a licence to manufacture "glass for glazing such as is made in France, Burgundy, and Lorraine." Carré imported his gentlemen glass-makers to make glass in the Weald and teach others the craft. He also tried to make crystal glass at the Crutched Friars Works in London with similar workers, but was not successful in this enterprise until he had employed Italians, notably Jacopo Verzelini.

Timber was being rapidly consumed in both glass and iron-production, and the Lorrainers began their trek in search of new woods through Hampshire, Gloucestershire, Severn Valley, branching out into north and south Staffordshire, Shropshire, Lancashire, Yorkshire, and Scotland. Then came the famous edict of 1615 which forbade the use of timber for firing furnaces. Coal was the only alternative, and no longer could glass-workers follow the woods (before the days of canals, railways, and good roads) but were obliged to stay where either pit or sea coal was available.

Coal was already being used for melting glass by workers at or near Greensforge, Kingswinford, in south Staffordshire, a few miles north of Stourbridge. To this district came the Lorrainers—the De

Hennezels, Thysacs, Thietrys, and Houx, names later to become anglicized as Henzey, Tyzack, Tyttery, and Hoe—with variations. They specialized in "broad" glass, made by blowing a cylinder of glass, slitting it along the top while hot, and flattening it under heat with a wooden paddle—the "slit-cylinder" method. Their rivals, the Normans, adopted the "crown" method. Here a bubble of glass was blown, then fixed to a pontil rod, the blowing iron broken off, and then, on the "punty" the bubble with the small hole where the iron had been broken off, was rotated rapidly in front of a flashing furnace until it suddenly opened out to form a flat disc something like four feet in diameter. When the "punty" was broken off this left a mark in the centre known as the "bullion" or "bulls-eye," now copied in some modern windows. Crown glass was more brilliant than broad, having a natural fire-polish. Both Broad and Crown glass came in and out of fashion.

While the window-glass and bottle industry was being carried on in various parts of Britain, the production of drinking glasses continued mainly in the London area. During the 17th century the granting of patents of monopolies was at the discretion of the Sovereign and the recipients were usually Court favourites. In 1615 Sir Edward Zouche had gained such a monopoly, but soon a partner in the enterprise, Admiral Sir Robert Mansell, set about gaining control of this monopoly. In 1623 Mansell was granted a new patent to "use exercise practise sett up and put into use the arte feate and misterie of melting and makeing all manner of drinking glasses broad glasses window glasses and all other kinds of glasses. . .with sea cole pitt coale or any other fewell whatsoever not being tymber or wood."

Thus glass-making is recognised as an art, a skill, and a craft. ("Misterie" in the above context means "craft"—the old Mystery plays were so called because they were performed by craftsmen).

Mansell thus gained control of both sides of the English glass industry, as well as exploiting the coal and clay industries, He certainly used Stourbridge clay to make his pots in which glass was melted.

For practically one hundred years London produced Venetian style drinking glasses, made by Italians. But there came resentment against Venetian glass both home-made and imported which was subject to crizzling, "rotting and decay," as well as against the temperamental Italian workmen.

At this stage a most important figure in the history of glass making appears. George Ravenscroft, glass merchant and manufacturer, and amateur chemist, with Venice experience, had been experimenting for some years in the production of clear glass to resemble natural rock crystal. First using the old soda recipes, he then decided to try lead oxide, no doubt getting the idea from the lead glazes used by potters, and aided by the English translation by Christopher Merret (t) in 1662 of *Neri's L'Arte Vetraria*, first published in 1612. There was nothing new in the use of lead oxide in glass-making. The Egyptians had used it to make coloured glass; there was over 35% in their opaque red glass, while in Roman times red glass had 13% and green 7%. Previously in the 6th century B.C. Mesopotamia had over 22% in its red, and in blue over 15%.

Sponsored by the Glass Sellers Company of London, one of the chief sufferers from the defects of Venetian glass, and with the Royal Society taking a fatherly interest, Ravenscroft worked at the Savoy glass-house in London and at experimental works in Henley-on-Thames. Using too much "salts" (potash) at first his lead glass "crizzled," but striking a better balance of silica, lead, and potash, he achieved a finer quality lead crystal than ever before. In recognition of his achievement the Glass Sellers Company allowed Ravenscroft to mark his glasses with the famous raven's head seal. But his glass at this stage still had slight colour. Ravenscroft retired in 1678 and died in 1683. It was left to his associate at Henley, Hawley Bishopp, to improve and by 1681 create the near-perfect

English lead crystal glass. The formula, which included over 30% lead oxide, has varied very little in the last three centuries, a tribute to Ravenscroft and Bishopp.

A number of London glass-houses were soon making this new glass, and by the end of the century Newcastle, Bristol, Stourbridge, and Dublin, had followed suit. As mentioned in the introduction to this work, Stourbridge has been a glass making centre since the beginning of the 17th century at least, when Paul Tyzack set up his works within a mile of the town centre.

The glass trade has had to battle against many storms. From 1745 to 1845 there was the iniquitous tax on glass which severely hampered progress in England. There have been wars and economic crises. Glass firms rise and fall, whole districts such as Birmingham and Dudley ceased to make glass but in this book we trace the history of one still flourishing firm in a glass district with three centuries of tradition behind it.

FURTHER READING

There is a large collection of literature on glass and glass making. The following is a brief list of either standard or up to date works, normally available from booksellers or larger libraries. *References to further reading are also made in the text.*

General

Haynes, E.B. Glass through the ages. Pelican Books (Various editions).
Newman, H. An illustrated dictionary of glass. Thames & Hudson 1977.
Vose, R.H. Glass (Connoisseur Illustrated Guides) The Connoisseur 1975.
Weiss, G. The book of glass. Barrie & Jenkins. 1971.

European glass

Polak, A. Glass: its makers and its public. Weidenfield & Nicolson 1975.
Ray & Lee Grover European art glass. Tuttle, Rutland Vermont 1975.

English glass

Kenyon, G. H. The glass industry of the Weald. Leicester Univ. Press. 1967.
Thorpe, W. A. A history of English and Irish glass. 2 vols. Medici Society.
Thorpe, W. A. English glass; 3rd Ed. Black 1961.
Wakefield, H. Nineteenth century British glass. Faber 1961.

Stourbridge glass

Guttery, D.R. From broad glass to cut crystal: a history of the Stourbridge glass industry. Hill 1956.
Haden, H. J. Notes on the Stourbridge glass trade. Brierley Hill/Dudley Libraries. 1969 etc.
Haden, H. J. The Stourbridge glass industry of the 19th century. Black Country Society. 1971.
Northwood, J. (II). John Northwood: his contribution to the Stourbridge flint glass industry. Mark & Moody. 1958.

Thomas Webb the First

Wordsley

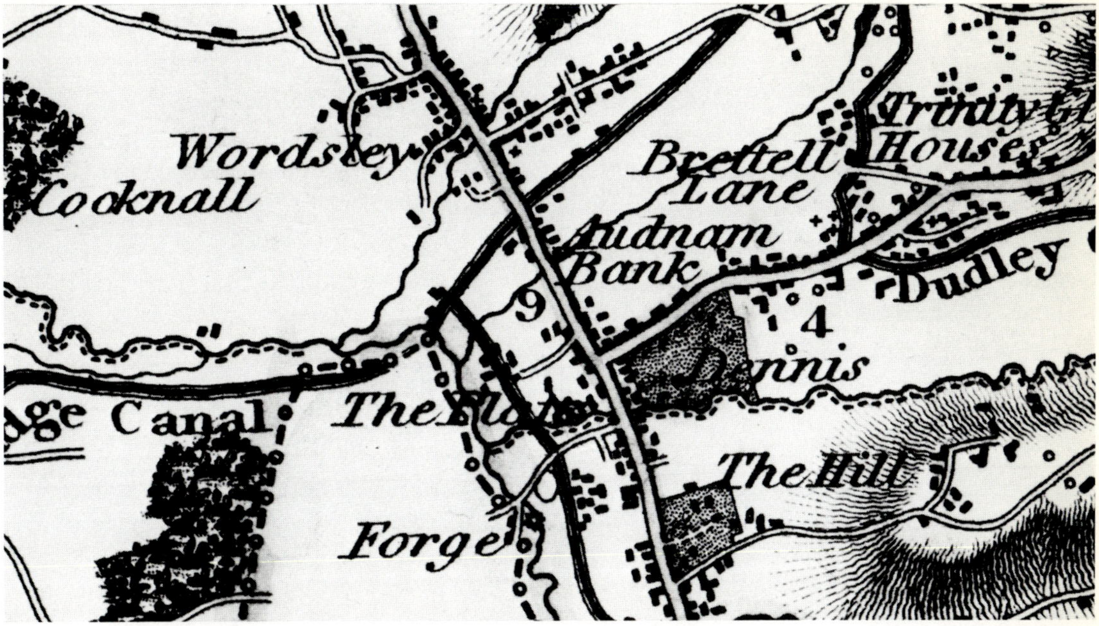

C. Greenwood's Staffordshire published June 1st 1820

Thomas Webb, founder of the firm which still bears his name after more than a century of distinction in the world of glass, was born at Stourbridge in Worcestershire on the 6th January, 1804. Like so many others famous in this great craft industry, he began his career in the Staffordshire village of Wordsley. Wordsley lies two miles north of Stourbridge and for most of the 19th century had a skyline dominated by a number of glass-house cones, some towering to almost 100 feet. On the main road from Stourbridge to Wolverhampton running through Wordsley by the canal side, were three glassworks adjoining each other—the White House, the Red House and the Wordsley Flint glassworks, this last at one time known also as "the London House" because it supplied the trade of that city.

Here Thomas Webb became initiated in the "art, feat and mystery" of glass-making. Benjamin Richardson the First, "father of the Stourbridge glass trade," records[1] how he and his brother William Haden Richardson acquired the Wordsley Flint Glassworks from the Wainwright brothers and that Benjamin Webb, a builder at The Dock in Wordsley, "hearing how things were," told the Richardsons that his brother John Webb, a Stourbridge farmer and butcher, had a son Thomas then aged 25, who would like to go into the glass trade. On the 25th December, 1829 an agreement was signed between the two Richardsons and Thomas Webb, creating the firm of Webb and Richardsons. The partnership was to last for almost seven years.

During this period, Thomas Webb's father also entered the industry. In July 1833 he became a partner of John Shepherd at the White House Works, trading as "Shepherd and Webb." Presumably this was the John Shepherd who originated from the West Country and worked for a time at Rufford and Walker's glassworks, The Heath, Stourbridge.[2] John Webb died in January 1835, leaving his share of the business to Thomas, his only surviving child. As a result, the son thus had interests in two glass firms. The following year John Shepherd decided to retire; in June 1836 his partnership with Thomas Webb was dissolved and Thomas bought John Shepherd's share in the business for £2,500. The firm, however, continued as "Shepherd and Webb," John Shepherd allowing his name to be used. For his services and for interest on his capital, he received £300 per annum.[3]

Benjamin Richardson mentions that Thomas Webb could have continued as a partner at the Wordsley Flint Glassworks, but comments that he "preferred to be with John Shepherd." It is more likely that his responsibilities at the White House following his partner's retirement caused Thomas to decide to concentrate his efforts there. By mutual agreement he parted from the Richardson brothers to be paid out "over £7,000."[4]

(It is interesting to note that in 1842 the Richardsons were joined by a third brother, Jonathan, to begin the famous firm of W. H., B. and J. Richardson, and that the successor to this Henry G. Richardson and Sons became absorbed in the firm of Thomas Webb and Sons, thus completing a full cycle).

The Platts

Soon after 1836, Thomas Webb decided to build himself new works adjoining Platts House, in Amblecote, a Georgian mansion previously the residence of John Pidcock, a partner in the nearby Dial Glassworks, on the east side of the Stourbridge Canal at Audnam, Wordsley. John Pidcock was a nephew of Joshua Henzey a descendant of the Huguenot Henzey's who had settled in the district early in the 17th century and, as so often occurred, he married into another glassmaking family—Mary daughter of Robert Honeyborne who operated a glass works at Brierley Hill, just over a mile distant. With its boundaries adjacent to Stourbridge and Wordsley, Amblecote lay in Staffordshire, between the town and village, but still within the extensive parish of Oldswinford, in the Diocese of Worcester. An agreement dated 5th December, 1837 between Shepherd and Webb and a glass-maker, Benjamin Chamberlain, regarding the loan of £5, was actually signed at the Platts by Thomas Webb, indicating that he was living there at that time.[5]

Engraving of The Platts Glassworks, from "Art Union" of 1846.

The date of the move from the White House works to the Platts can be determined by two agreements in an Apprentices' Book preserved at the Dennis Glassworks. One of these binds Benjamin Harrop, glass servitor on 20th June 1840, to John Shepherd and Thomas Webb, of *Wordsley*. The two parties in the next agreement, drawn up on 27th November 1840, are Edward Ashton, glassmaker and Thomas Webb, *The Platts.* Both agreements are signed by Thomas Webb and witnessed by Joseph Webb, clerk to the firm. Evidently the use of John Shepherd's name ceased before the end of the agreed five years when Thomas Webb left Wordsley.

The Apprentices' Book is a valuable record regarding wages and other conditions of work in the glass trade around the middle of the 19th century. The first agreement in the book, dated October 1836, is interesting. It is between John Shepherd and Thomas Webb, and John Perry, Servitor. The two partners "will pay or cause to be paid unto the said John Perry the weekly wages or sum of thirteen shillings per week for every eleven moves or work which he the said John Perry shall do, make, or perform during the week, and the farther wages or sum of fifteen pence for every extra or additional move over and above the said eleven moves which he shall make, do, or perform in any one week for the first year." In the second year the wages rose to fifteen shillings a week, and in the third year to sixteen.

Overtime payments increased from fifteen pence per move to seventeen pence. Apart from more money in his pocket John Perry received also an extra for his head—a new hat. The hat was, however, more of a status symbol than a sartorial embellishment!

The 1851 Census records show Thomas Webb as living at Platts House, a widower with his five sons and two daughters. In 1833, he had married Elizabeth Heming (daughter of a Stourbridge printer in a substantial way of business) who died in December 1849. Also in the household was Maria Heming his sister-in-law, a governess, and three servants.

In an article in *The Art Union* (later *The Art Journal*) of April 1846, the writer describes his visit to the Platts Works. "Cleanliness and comfort are apparent everywhere; the work people healthy and content; while even so adjacent to furnaces, ever burning, nature is not only permitted to wear the garb of refreshing green, but lawns and trees, and elegant parterres exhibit that taste and care for the beautiful which cannot fail to influence the presiding mind of the place." The accompanying engraving certainly shows a rather stately Platts House in pleasant rural surroundings not altogether marred by the works chimneys. The writer continues: "Mr. Webb devotes his attention chiefly, if not exclusively, to the manufacture of flint-glass; and it is only justice to him to state that, in clearness and purity, he is confessedly unsurpassed in Europe. Hence, much of his produce goes to the creation of chandeliers, candelabras, and objects in which the quality alluded to is of the highest importance." There are tributes to some of the glass made at the Platts, with attractive engraved illustrations; a claret jug "bold and massive: the artist has designed with judgement, and the mechanic has cut with vigour," a decanter "so exquisitely beautiful in shape and delicate in execution." As well as illustrations of a "very elegant water-jug, an adaptation from Etruscan," a butter cooler "a fine example of cutting" and a group of table glasses, there is a picture of "a salad-bowl, so constructed as to form a celery bowl, and to act as either without impairing its form. It will be obvious that, by reversing the object, we substitute its new character for that which it previously sustained. It may form also an elegant ornament for the drawing room—of which it is every way worthy—to contain flowers. An object more refreshing to mind and eye, in any position, it would be difficult to find."

There is mention of a report by a factory inspector, R. H. Horne. "The works of Mr. Thomas Webb (hamlet of Amblecote, in Old Swinford), which rank with the largest Glass Works in the Kingdom, for their perfect state of repair, extreme cleanliness, careful boxing or railing off of dangerous machines, and special provisions, may stand as a model for all similar works." Thus we see high praise for Thomas Webb the First both as a manufacturer of glass and as an employer of men.

By 1851 Thomas Webb was producing both flint and coloured glass as well as iron founding. At the Great Exhibition of that year his firm displayed "various patterns of glass, consisting of bowls and pedestals, dishes, sweetmeats, sugars and cream bowls, butters, ice-pails, plates and floats; pine stands, jugs, goblets, decanters, wines, liqueurs, fingers, coolers, tumblers, ales, salts, mustards, pickles, custards, jellies, soda goblets, flower vases, toilettes, pedestal lamps, &c."

In his notes, Ben Richardson reveals that just after 1851 Thomas Webb, who was also somewhat unprofitably in business locally as an iron founder was in some financial difficulties, and that mainly for this reason he decided to move from the Platts. (The Platts Works was afterwards operated by the Stourbridge Sheet and Crown Glass Co. Limited). For a short while the works was leased and operated by a Samuel Bowen who earlier had failed as a glass manufacturer at Nailsea. At first he managed to undercut the flat glass price fixed by the principal manufacturers but before long he found he was unable to compete with the flat glass producers such as the Hartleys (who, in fact had acquired the Platts glassworks), the Pilkingtons and the Chances, and was again bankrupt. Subsequently, the Platts works was bought by Chance of Smethwick who operated it for a short boom period in the 1870's and then closed it down.

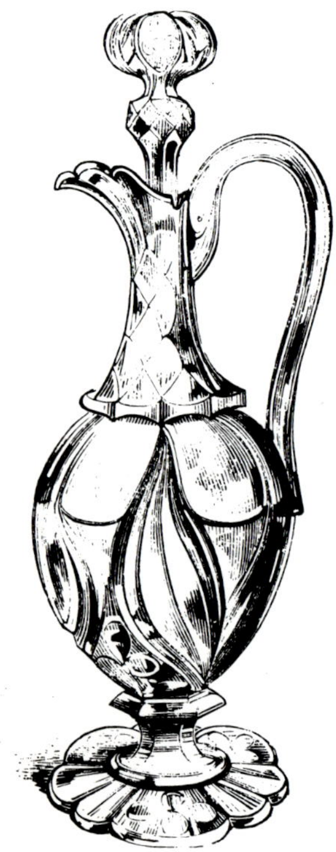

A Platts claret jug and salad bowl

Dennis

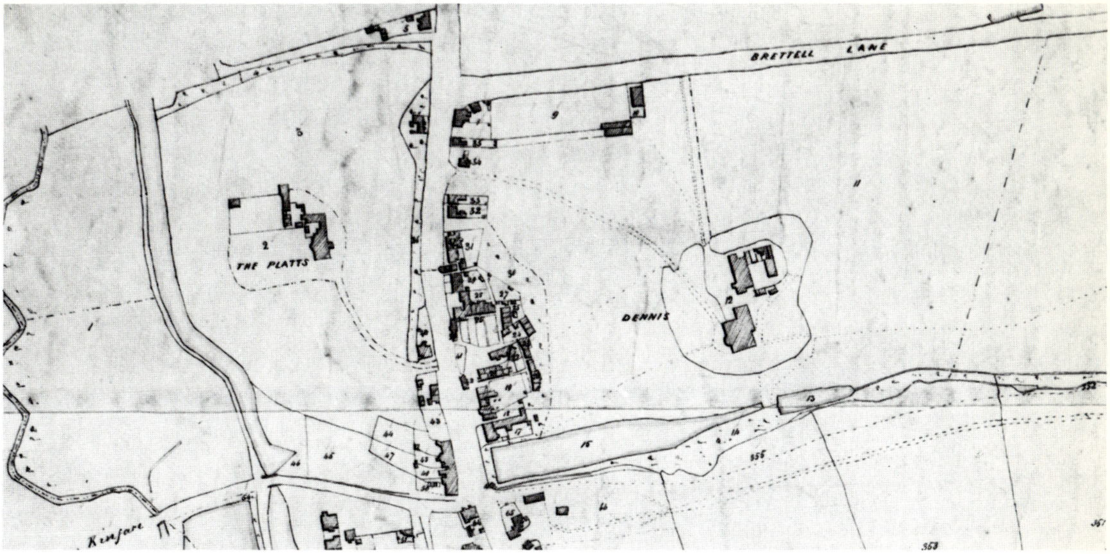

Section of the Tithe Map for Amblecote dated 1839.

Apart from the Apprentices' Book, Dennis Glass Works has another interesting record—a book giving details of pots purchased and in most cases how long they lasted. These were the clay pots in which the "batch" for making glass was melted. This book was begun at the Platts in 1852, but in August 1855 entries are headed "Dennis Glass Works," listing 13 pots acquired from 21st August to 10th September. Ten of these pots were obtained from Squires, pot makers in nearby Brettell Lane, the family carrying on the business until recent years.

The Dennis Glass Works, known also as the Stourbridge Glass Works during the latter part of the 19th century, was built at the rear of Dennis Hall in Dennis Park, Amblecote. The Park at that time extended from the main Stourbridge-Wolverhampton road over a wide area to beyond what is now the upper part of Collis Street to Brettell Lane, but the Park is now covered mainly by housing development. The name "Dennis" has its origins at least as far back as the 14th century, when Walter de Denys, or Water the Dane, was "Regarder of the King's Forest." This forest, The Royal Forest of Kinver, was extensive but unfortunately its boundaries described in the Perambulation of 1300 are not altogether recognisable. Within the Forest originally were Kinver itself, Lower Penn (near Wolverhampton), Seisdon, Wombourn, Swindon, parts of Himley, Kingswinford, Amblecote, Wordsley, Pedmore, Wollaston, Arley and villages near Kidderminster.

The new works was built on a site which had been used for glass making at intervals since the end of the 17th century. One of the Batchelor family, who had been with Paul Henzey, broad glass-maker at Brettell, moved to Dennis in 1691 to make bottles[6] In an indenture dated 1st March, 1738, preserved at Dennis Glass Works, there are mentions of previous leases of 1691 and 1714. Charles Fox of Chacombe Priory, leased to Humphrey Batchelor, an Amblecote glass-maker, "all that Messuage or tenement wherein the said Thomas Bradley did formerly dwell and all the Glasshouse heretofore in the tenure of the said Thomas Bradley and also all those Four Closes or inclosures of arrable meadow or pasture ground conteyning by Estimation Five and Thirty Acres or thereabouts be the same more or less commonly called or known by the name of Dennis..."

Also leased is "that Messuage or dwelling house with the Outhouses garden Foldyard backside and appurtenances late in the Occupation of the Said John Bradley and all that Glasshouse heretofore in the holding of Jeremia Minors and Edward Bradley and since used by the said John Bradley for making of White glass together with the sroare two warehouses two pott chambers, one stable and all other Outhouses, Edifices and buildings....". (The sroare, or shrower is that part of the works where the annealed glass is taken from the lear).

Thus it is apparent that there were two glass-works on the Dennis estate. In 1728 an agreement mentions the White House or fimbrell glass house. This agreement between Humfrey Bachelor and Henry Barrar, requires that the latter should leave "a new furnace with two good spreading plates, a pot arch and two other Arches and a Chalker for burning."

(Spreading plates were the plates on which "broad-glass" was flattened, a stage in the Lorraine method of making window glass in which a cylinder of glass was blown, slit, opened and then flattened. A pot arch was the arch in which a clay pot used for melting glass was heated before being transferred to the furnace. "Other arches" would be arches in which glass was annealed. A chalker, or calcar, was the place in which sand was heated to dry it and to get rid of combustible matter.

There are no known records which reveal for how much longer glass was made at Dennis during the 18th century, or what "white" glass was produced in that period.

The Dennis estate eventually passed from the Bradleys to the Hill family who were connected by marriage to the Batchelors. The Hills had important connections with the glass and iron trades at Stourbridge, as well as banking interests in the district. They were partners, for instance, with Ensell at Coalbournhill glass-works, later taken over by Joseph Webb and now the home of Webb-Corbett Limited. It was Thomas Hill who built Dennis House in the 1770's, a residence which later became Dennis Hall and eventually the offices of Thomas Webb and Sons. Thomas Hill, squire of Dennis Park, had the derelict glass-works within his grounds demolished and used the bricks to build the first school at Lye near Stourbridge. He had invested heavily in an ironworks at Blaenavon, retired and died there in 1827. The house was later occupied by the Wheeley family, a family involved in the glass, coal and iron trades of the district.

The Hall eventually came into the possession of William Blow Collis, a Stourbridge solicitor, who offered it for sale in 1845 for use as a hospital, but although a public meeting was in favour of the scheme, it was found that there were insufficient funds to carry out the project.

The 1851 Census reveals that Dennis Hall was then tenanted by John Grier, M.A., born in Ireland, at that time Incumbent of Amblecote and Chaplain of the Kingswinford Union Workhouse at Wordsley.

In 1839, when William Seagar Wheeley had been the owner of 41 acres of land in Dennis Park, including the Hall, the Tithe Commissioners confirmed the apportionment of rent charges. By June 1856 the land had come into the possession of George Robinson, Thomas Webb, Jeremiah Mathews, William Blow Collis, Elizabeth King (widow) and Edward King Perrens, George King Harrison, Edward Westwood (trustees under the will of William King deceased). Some of these names are of well-known local figures. It is interesting to note that the new street running from the turnpike road parallel with Brettell Lane to the top part of Collis Street was later named after William King—but in reverse. The main entrance to Dennis Glass Works is now in King William Street. The 1856 revised apportionment of rents revealed that Thomas Webb owned and occupied just over 4 acres which included House, Manufactory, Lands and Gardens, and over 1 acre of coppice and land for which rent due to the Rector was £4.8s.3d per annum.

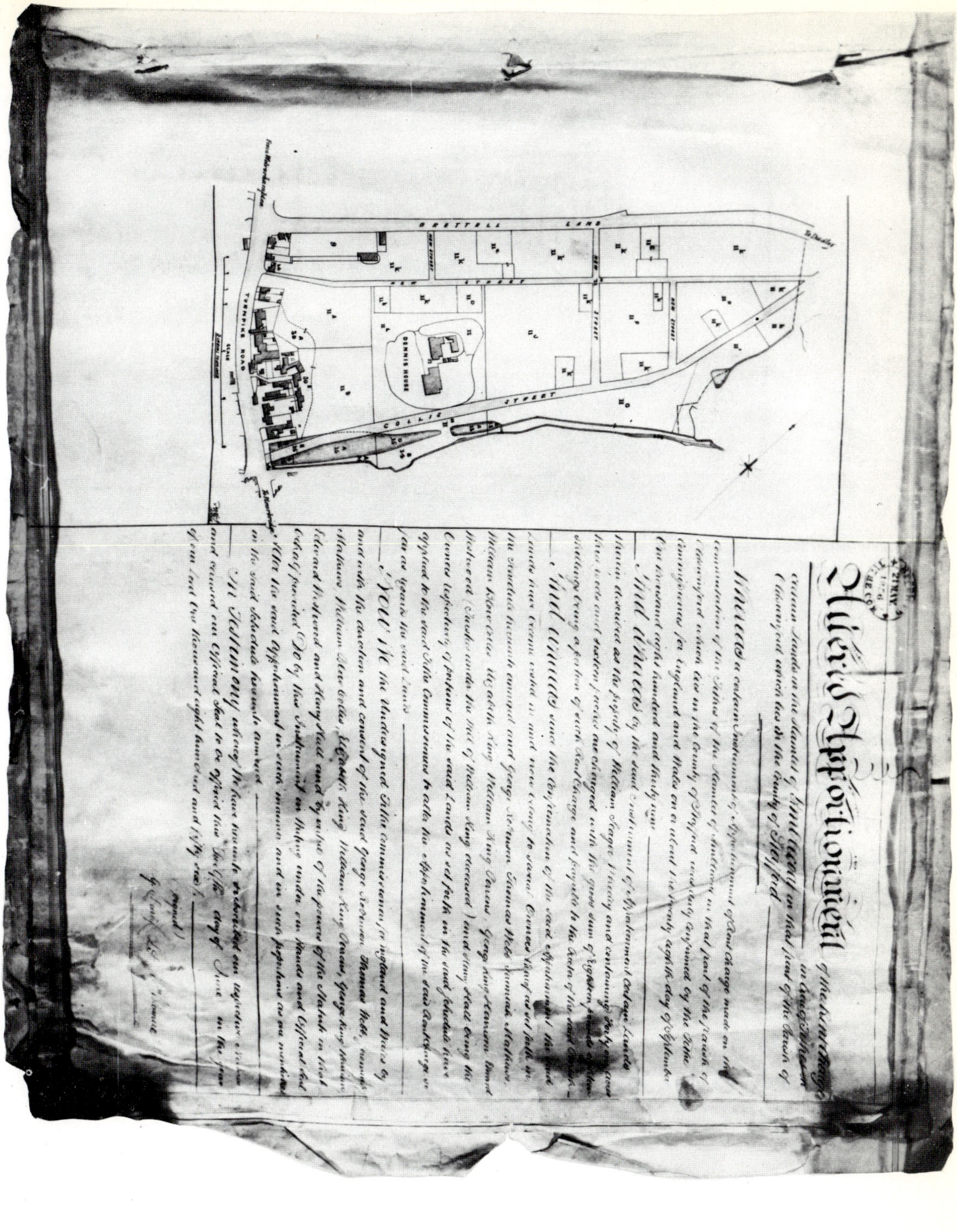

Revised apportionment of rents, 1856

As already mentioned, by 1855 Thomas Webb was in occupation of Dennis Hall and had built a new glass-works at the rear. It is a significant fact that in those times glass manufacturers usually lived near to their works in order to keep a sharp eye on operations and the Dennis Glassworks actually adjoined its proprietor's home. Another milestone in the history of the firm is recorded again in the Apprentices' Book. On 23rd May 1859, an agreement with Henry Male, glass-maker, was signed by T. W. Webb (Thomas Wilkes Webb, son of Thomas Webb) on behalf of Thomas Webb *and Sons*, of Dennis.

On an invoice dated 14th November 1860 preserved at Dennis Glass Works to the printed name "Thomas Webb" a clerkly hand has added "& Sons," and to the printed "Dennis Glass Works, Stourbridge" the same hand has appended "& Ironfoundry." The bill head has an illustration of the Works at that time.

These two documents confirm that Thomas Webb the First, 51 years of age when he started glass-making at Dennis, had within four years brought sons into his now prosperous business. They were, in fact, Charles and Thomas Wilkes. When their father retired in 1863, the sons took charge and on their father's death in 1869, another brother, Walter Wilkes Webb, became the third partner.

Apart from his iron foundry at Dennis, Thomas Webb was also owner of an iron works in Brettell Lane. Father of eleven children, four of whom did not survive infancy, he retired to Herefordshire where he had acquired farms,—and when he died at Fern Hill on 14th December, 1869, these were bequeathed to his daughters.

As well as being known as the founder of a famous firm, Thomas Webb will also be remembered as the inventor of an important innovation—a circular lear (lehr), for which he was granted a patent in January 1854. It is most likely that although he was still at The Platts Glass Works, he experimented with the new lear at the Dennis Works under construction at that time.

The lear is described in the patent as "improved apparatus applicable to the annealing of glass and the firing of pottery."

When the Iron and Steel Institute held an annual meeting in Birmingham in 1895 it was reported that "one of the most interesting (excursions) was a visit to the glass manufactory of Messrs. Thomas Webb & Sons Limited at Stourbridge. The visitors were received by Messrs. Charles, Walter and Henry Webb who conducted them over the establishment and explained the various processes employed in the working of the many kinds of glass for which the firm is famous. Attention was directed to the circular lear believed to be the only one in use and which was invented by the late Mr. Webb, the founder of the firm."[7]

This circular lear with the obvious advantage of saving works space, was comparatively simple in design. The main part consisted of two large circles made of cast iron plates which revolved horizontally one within the other acting as conveyors. These were easily operated by two handles attached to gear wheels engaging with teeth underneath the circles. The arrangement was low geared and the circles on which the glass for annealing was placed, could be moved quite slowly, resting on wheels fixed to spindles.

Half the lear was in the glass house and the other half in the "shrower," the halves being separated by the glass-house wall. Near the centre of the lear, on the glass-house side, was a coal fired box. The glass passed through a hole in the wall (the entrance to a tunnel), then along the tunnel to be taken off the conveyor in the "shrower," ready for the decorator.

Although the firm used other lears during the 20th century, including a Teisen-coke/gas producer type, and the first one to be heated by town's gas, Thomas Webb's circular lear was still operating in the early 1930's after almost 80 years of practically trouble-free working.[8]

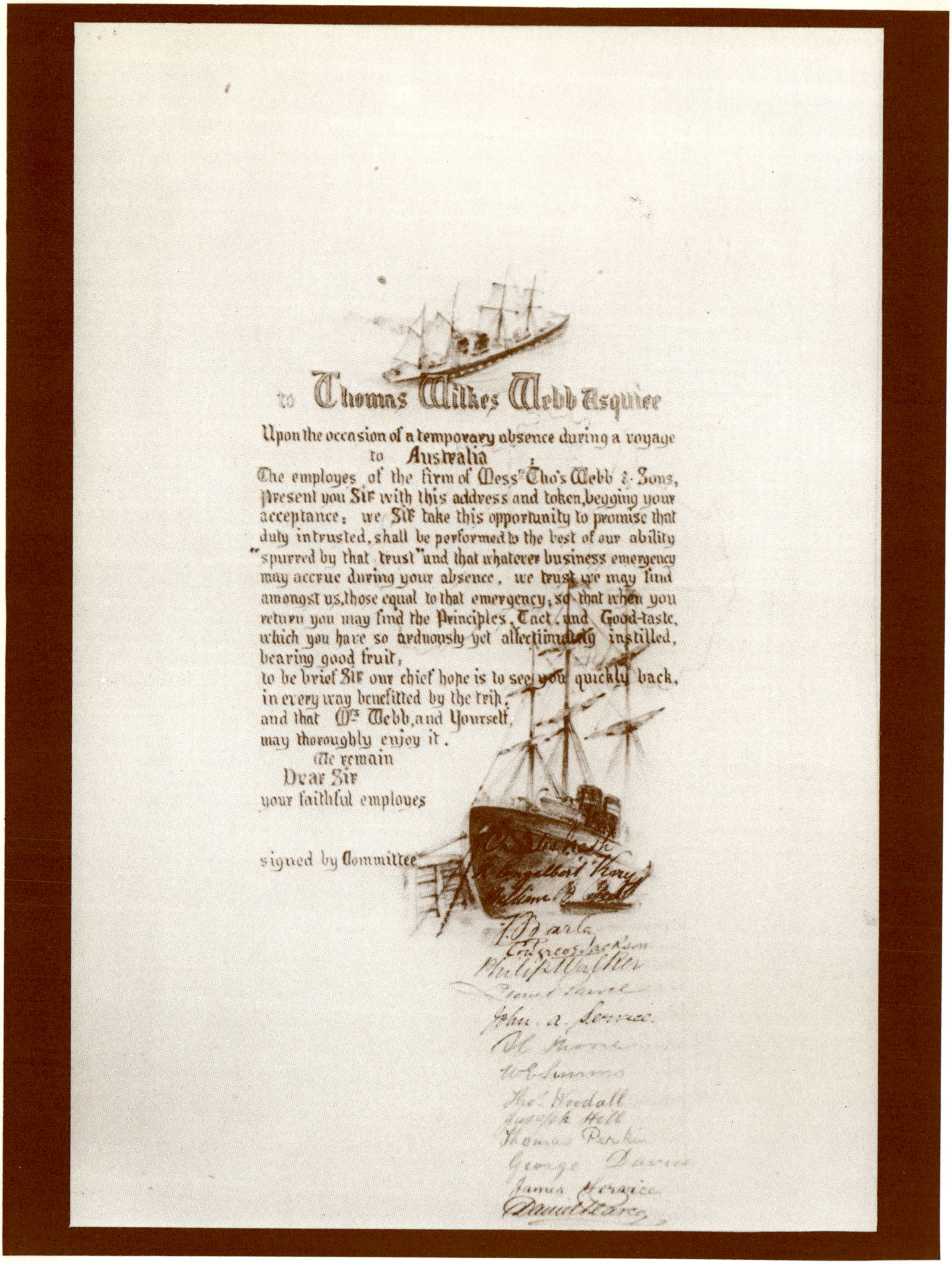

to Thomas Wilkes Webb Esquire

Upon the occasion of a temporary absence during a voyage to Australia

The employes of the firm of Messrs Tho's Webb & Sons, present you Sir with this address and token, begging your acceptance: we Sir take this opportunity to promise that duty intrusted, shall be performed to the best of our ability "spurred by that trust" and that whatever business emergency may accrue during your absence, we trust we may find amongst us, those equal to that emergency; so that when you return you may find the Principles, Tact, and Good-taste, which you have so arduously yet affectionately instilled, bearing good fruit;

to be brief Sir our chief hope is to see you quickly back, in every way benefitted by the trip, and that Mrs Webb, and Yourself, may thoroughly enjoy it.

We remain
Dear Sir
your faithful employes

signed by Committee

[illegible]
[illegible]
[illegible]
[illegible]
[illegible]
Philip Walker
[illegible]
John A. Lowe
[illegible]
W. E. Simmons
Thos. Woodall
Joseph Hill
Thomas Perkin
George Davies
James Horrace
[illegible]

Thomas Wilkes Webb

Of all the Webbs, Thomas Wilkes, Thomas Webb the Second, probably did most to make the firm internationally famous. Born in Stourbridge on 9th October, 1836 he left school at the age of fourteen and entered his father's employment as clerk at the Platts works. Five years after the 1855 move to Dennis, he became a partner in the firm. He set out at once to equal the finest continental glass in all aspects—the "metal" (glass) itself, colours, making and decorating.

Thomas Wilkes Webb not only thought out new ideas but was able to put them into practice, giving his workmen practical advice and encouragement. A great deal of time and money was spent on development and craftsmen were brought over from Bohemia and France to help. Thomas travelled extensively as an ambassador for his firm, to search for new ideas, and for craftsmen. One particular journey is pleasantly commemorated by a goodwill message from his employees, showing with what great affection he was regarded. That was his visit to Australia in 1884.

In a later chapter, an account will be given of the fine glass produced at Dennis under Thomas Wilkes Webb's direction. Suffice it is to mention at this point, firstly the cameo glass decorated by the world's greatest craftsmen, developing from simple floral patterns to portrayals of the human figure; and secondly "Burmese" glass for which Thomas purchased the recipe during a visit to the United States. Apart from the development of coloured glasses, Thomas saw his firm's increasing fame as producers of high quality crystal glass, including "Rock Crystal." As mentioned in the section on Webb glass, a number of patents appeared in his name. One not mentioned, however, is that of 1867 for "Shell components, especially feet."

Webb glass was on show at a number of exhibitions, both in this country and abroad. In 1876 the Worshipful Company of Glass Sellers organised an exhibition at the Alexandra Palace, London, "to encourage competition and improvements in the manufacture of glass" at which two Webb engravers, Frederick Engelbert Kny and William Fritsche were awarded Bronze Medals. During the same year, in June 1876, Thomas Wilkes Webb obtained a patent for "Improvements in the manufacture of ornamental vases and other articles of glass."

The firm's greatest achievement came two years later. At the 1878 Paris International Exhibition they were awarded the Grand Prix for glass. For the head of the firm there was a personal distinction —the Legion of Honour from the French government. With typical modesty Thomas Wilkes wished this to be conferred on brother Charles, who declined. The official Illustrated Catalogue described the firm in glowing terms.

"MESSRS. THOMAS WEBB & CO., of Stourbridge, are the best makers of Crystal Glass in England, and consequently, in the world; for if Germany and France surpass us in the production of coloured glass, they are far behind us in the pure metal, worked or unworked. Messrs. Webb have long been renowned for supremacy in diamond cutting; in the examples they now show of designing and engraving they compete with the best manufacturers of the Continent—excelled by none of them."

1878.

Webb glass in the Exhibition was wide ranging. Apart from forty or fifty cases of larger items which had already been sent, a representative of the "Birmingham Daily Gazette" had a preview of exhibition items and his account appeared on 11th April, 1878.

"For purity of form and metal nothing could surpass the claret jugs and decanters, the water jugs and goblets" he writes. He was impressed by glass in the Venetian style and the cased glass using particularly opal, lemon, ruby, pink and blue colours. Also outstanding were the cut crystal and coloured services designed by Charles Webb.

A Dennis "Queen Anne" chandelier.

Another famous craftsman, Daniel Pearce was responsible for the design and erection of the Webb stand as well as for two chandeliers which made impressive centre pieces. Daniel Pearce had been connected with the London firm, Dobson & Pearce, later Phillips and Pearce. Fortunately, these chandeliers can still be seen at Dennis Hall. The one in the entrance hall to Webb's offices is a Venetian air-twist chandelier now reduced to 36 lights, while the other over the main staircase is a wonderful example of brilliant cut crystal glass, having 27 lights incorporating many hundreds of pieces.

George Augustus Henry Sala (1828-1895) a well known writer of his day, especially as a contributor to the Illustrated London News, and Household Words, also pays tribute to Webb glass of this period. Referring to French glass, he mentions this as "lacking what diamond merchants call 'show' and compared with that of Webb's glass, the brilliance of its 'water' is as the brilliance of gas compared with electric light."

Thomas Wilkes was interested not only in Webb glass. He had followed closely John Northwood's progress in reviving the art of cameo glass, and when the famous Northwood replica of the Portland Vase was completed in 1876, he immediately commissioned John to execute a piece of cameo glass for the firm. John Northwood's firm, J. & J. Northwood of Wordsley had been doing etching for Webb's. John Northwood I eventually became Works Manager at Stevens and Williams Limited, of Moor Lane, Brierley Hill, one of Thomas Webb and Sons principal competitors in producing art glass.

The commissioned glass was to become known as the Dennis or Pegasus Vase and is now in the Smithsonian Institution, Washington. The covered vase is a magnificent example of cameo-glass made of dark blue glass cased with 'opal' glass. The finial on the cover is solid 'opal' carved to represent Pegasus, the mythical flying horse. The ovoid body has two solid horses' head handles and a carved frieze, on the one side of which is Venus and on the other Aurora with a number of other figures.

A fine tribute was paid to Thomas Wilkes by one of Webb's greatest craftsmen, George Woodall. "Mr. Webb was really the cause of the revival of the glass trade which was seen in and about the early eighties. The leading spirit of the trade; he had a marvellous belief in what the trade could do. He was not only an artist but he knew the trade thoroughly technically and in other ways. He knew exactly what the public wanted and encouraged his men in every possible way in the right direction."[9]

In November 1886 the firm became a public company. The prospectus was issued on the 18th of the month and the subscription list closed five days later.[10] The share capital was £100,000 in 20,000 shares of £5 each. Additionally, of £30,000 worth of 5 per cent. First Mortgage Debentures were offered, redeemable at the Company's option after five years, at 5 per cent premium. Thomas Wilkes and brother Charles became Managing Directors, with Clement F. Wedgwood also on the Board. The brother, Walter Wilkes, retired from the business. The actual purchase money was £110,000 and the two senior partners, as vendors, bound themselves to act as Managing Directors for five years and receive for their services a yearly salary of £500 each to be doubled when the Company's net profits exceeded 10 per cent a year on the paid up capital. The Company agreed to lease a dwelling house" (presumably Dennis Hall) to Charles Webb.

At the time the property in Amblecote sold to the Company by the firm comprised about 12 acres of freehold land, upon which stood the Dennis (or Stourbridge) Glass Works, together with extensive offices, stock and showrooms, houses for the manager and workmen, Dennis Hall itself, with some leasehold property adjoining, also engines, plant machinery and utensils used in the business, all valued at £45,300. The value of the stock at various places of business was assessed at just over £40,090. Thirdly, £21,609 was the valuation figure for existing contracts, letters patent, trade secrets, registered designs for shapes, decorations and other patterns. Included in this third figure were the firm's leasehold premises in Charterhouse Street, London and wholesale and retail warehouse in Collins Street East, Melbourne, Australia, and also the goodwill of the business.

An 1889 advertisement in the Pottery Gazette subsequently proclaims the range of Webb products.

Unfortunately, Thomas Wilkes Webb was not to complete his initial five years as Managing Director. No doubt his untiring efforts brought ill health and a comparatively early death at the age of 54 years. He died at his home, The Mount in Stourbridge on the 1st January 1891 and was buried in the town's cemetery. He had lived previously at The Birches, Hagley. The second Thomas Webb was a Justice of the Peace for Staffordshire and a strong supporter of the local Volunteer Movement. Otherwise, his life and efforts were devoted to the trade to which he brought such distinction. He was greatly esteemed and mourned by a wide circle of friends, both within the glass trade and outside, particularly by leading figures in the art world.[11]

In 1864 he had married Helen Constance Carter. Their family consisted of Thomas (the Third) who became an original partner of Thomas Webb and Corbett at the White House works at Wordsley in 1897; Charles Walter Herbert who took his elder brother's place as head of the Webb-Corbett firm in 1903 when the former retired; and two daughters—Hilda and May.

REFERENCES

1. Manuscript notes by Ben Richardson I in possession of the author.
2. Ibid.
3. Information supplied by Mr. H. J. Haden from indenture.
4. Richardson notes.
5. Apprentices' book at Dennis Hall (see text following).
6. D. R. Guttery. From Broad-glass to cut crystal.
7. Pottery Gazette, 1895.
8. Information supplied by Mr. S. R. Eveson.
9. County Express, Stourbridge, 20th January 1912.
10. Pottery Gazette, December 1886.
11. Obituary. Pottery Gazette, February 1891.

The Twentieth Century

In 1900, when Charles Webb retired, another of the firm's notabilities appears as Managing Director. Congreve William Jackson was to hold this important post for twenty years. Jackson had been the firm's traveller during the 1880's and London Agent during the 1890's. He set about restoring the Company's finances, which had deteriorated largely on account of the partners' policy of producing a too extensive range of decorative glass-ware, costly to make and difficult to sell profitably. In 1908 Thomas Webb and Sons staged a spectacular show at the Franco British Exhibition held at the White City in Shepherd's Bush, London where, not content with the normal display of products, they built a small glass-house and from a three tiered platform the public, for the sum of 6d, were able to see all stages of making and decorating glass.

Each day skilled workers demonstrated the making of a wine glass or a vase and even permitted the spectator to blow fantastic shapes. A pamphlet describing the processes and a set of post cards illustrating them were issued.

Franco-British Exhibition, 1908.

At this exhibition, in the Furniture and Decorative Arts building, there was a comprehensive display of Webb glass. "Amongst the specimens of cut glass with which the tables are laden are pieces of great value showing beautiful rock crystal effects . . . Quite the newest thing is the development of the Chippendale and Adams schemes in glass in order that harmony may be complete in rooms furnished in these styles."

The cut glass was designed by James R. Service and Lionel Pearce, and made under the supervision of foreman E. Parrish. Lionel Pearce also designed a show piece—the remarkable "Polar Vase," as well as two cut glass cannons. Apart from this fine display of crystal glass, were three George Woodall pieces "The Dance," "Cupid's Shrine" and "The Wild Wave." Jules Barbe's gilt and enamel decoration was also represented as well as the engraved work of William Fritsche.

A more light hearted note was struck by the production of glass animals and the sale of glass pigs and teddy-bears with other souvenirs. Some of these, including a hat pin and pigs made by Albert Saunders, were given to Queen Alexandra when she visited the White City. Webb's "Glass Furnace" had 150,000 visitors.

In the same year at the same place the Imperial International Exhibition was held. Webbs gaining a Grand Prix for "Cut, engraved and sculptured glass."

Then came the Great War of 1914-18 when the firm's production was limited to plain glass-ware and electric light bulbs. The English glass trade was one of the many casualties of this tragic and frustrating era, indeed, the trade was never to recover completely. So many skilled makers and decorators were lost during the economic aftermath that it was impossible to replace them completely.

On 25th June, 1920 the firm became incorporated as a limited private Company under the name of "THOS. WEBB AND SONS LIMITED." It then became part of a new Company Webb's Crystal Glass Co. Limited, to be joined by the Edinburgh and Leith Flint Glass Co. (which in 1955 became the Edinburgh Crystal Glass Co.). In 1920 Congreve Jackson retired.

In the early 1920's the firm (jointly with Stevens & Williams) purchased the assets of Guest Brothers Etching Works in Brettell Lane. Guest's had previously done etching for Webb's.

In the early 1930's, the old established firm of Henry G. Richardson & Sons was acquired by Webb's, who continued to produce Richardson patterns at Dennis trading them under the Richardson name. Mr. Ben Richardson died in 1956.

The early 1930's saw serious trade depression throughout the country, with the crystal glass industry suffering badly. Several small local glassworks were compelled to close down during this period of trade slump for they found it impossible to compete in the British market with imported glass from the Continent where glass workers' wages were substantially lower and production higher. The Webb Company could scarcely have chosen a better leader than they did in 1932 when Carl Gottwald Sven Harald Fogelberg from Sweden, was appointed General Manager of Webb's Crystal. Here was a man of great technical and organising ability who was to help steer the Company away from financial disaster and place it on the path to prosperity.

Sven Fogelberg's grandfather, J. A. Gottwald Fogelberg was book-keeper, later Manager of the Swedish Kosta Glassworks. His father Carl was Managing Director from 1905 until 1926 when Sven succeeded him, a post he occupied until coming to England in 1932. Under his direction an essential modernisation programme was carried out both at Dennis and Edinburgh. In 1933 the furnaces for glass melting were converted from coal to oil-firing. This meant a shorter melting time and increased productivity. The lehrs and pot-arches were changed to town-gas firing.

Fogelberg then introduced new glass-making techniques with the help of glass-makers from Sweden, Holland, Czechoslovakia and Germany. The Company had just begun to feel the benefits from all these changes when the Second World War broke out.

During the 1939-1945 war period the production of all forms of table and art glass was very restricted, but Fogelberg successfully guided the Company into producing, as well as utility ware, industrial glass for radar, X-rays and later for television, so successfully in fact that Dennis Glassworks continued making some of these types after the War.

Sven was appointed Managing Director of Webb's Crystal Glass Company in 1955. In the showroom can be seen the "Connoisseur" service attributed to him, which won the Design of the Year Award in 1957. He retired in 1963 and died suddenly at his Hagley home on 10th May, 1971.

Mr. Stanley R. Eveson, who joined Webb's as a boy in 1929 and was Technical Director until his retirement in April 1978, describes briefly almost a half-century's progress:

"When I joined, to learn the technical side of the business, we were just entering a very difficult period."

"The demand for very expensive and richly cut ware was diminishing because people did not have the money to buy this type of luxury product. This meant that the firm had to employ some of its skilled men on making less expensive glassware. When serious unemployment came in the early 1930's the Company had to discharge skilled glassmakers, decorators and staff and put on short time, many of those who remained.

"Technical difficulties associated with the glass furnaces meant that, up to 1933 glassmakers could not work on Mondays. They made up their 48 hour week by starting at 6 a.m. on Tuesdays and working a two six-hour shift system through to 6 a.m. on Saturdays.

"In those days working conditions in the glasshouse were difficult, to put it mildly, but from the 1930's onwards emphasis given to technical development resulted in better working conditions. "Furnaces previously fired by coal were converted to oil firing in 1933. This reduced the melting time drastically, provided greater output from the same capacity and meant we could maintain our existing prices while competitors increased theirs. Shortly before 1939, we were in a position to make technical glass and by coincidence we were asked to try making heat resisting glass for the electronic industry. Although we did not know at the time, we made a large proportion of the valve envelopes for radar purposes during the war. We were also asked to make Lead Glass X-ray tubes when there was a shortage of them for mobile units for Russia.

"Gradually, with increased prosperity after the war, more skilled men returned to the industry and a period of progress began.

"However, there remained the difficulty of getting on with major technical redevelopment which was sorely needed because of our old buildings and plant, particularly in the decorating and warehousing department.

"In 1964 acquisition by Crown House Limited brought modernisation from a dream to a possibility."

Dema and Crown House

In the year 1971, Webb's Crystal Glass Co. Limited was merged with Dema Glass Limited, the principal table glassware subsidiary of Crown House Limited.

Dema's Chairman, Mr. R. S. Uffindell, has kindly supplied the following notes:—

"I joined Dema Glass Limited in 1945 and was appointed Managing Director in 1952 on the death of my co-founder of the business. During the period from 1945 to 1952 Dema was trading as a merchant concerned with hand made and machine made table glassware, the major part of the sales being to the chain store market in the United Kingdom.

"From 1952 the Company expanded the sales of the machine made glassware to the licensed victualler and catering trade in the United Kingdom and to many overseas markets.

"In 1963, the Dema management decided that a manufacturing base and brand name was important if the Company were to remain and to expand as a major supplier of table glassware; the result was the acquisition by Crown House Limited in 1964 of Webbs Crystal Glass Co. Limited which included two crystal factories namely Thos. Webb & Sons and Edinburgh Crystal.

"Since then, the Company has pursued a policy of substantial investment in plant and buildings at both factories in an endeavour to improve the somewhat Dickensian working conditions which were apparent in 1964. It was hoped that the material improvements in conditions would encourage younger people into the business and improve efficiency.

"The Company has benefited from its association with a fine quality product and the factory has in turn been able to retain a dignified and worthwhile craft.

"During my 14 years relationship with Thos. Webb & Sons, it has brought me much pleasure, many disappointments and has always been a source of challenge and great interest."

Mr. E. A. Stott, Managing Director, continues the story:
"I was Company Secretary of Crown House Limited when it acquired Webbs Crystal Glass Co. Limited. In 1965 I moved to the Glass Division of Crown House, Webb's in particular, and have found it a thoroughly fascinating industry. It is, in my opinion, an industry which can be very exhilarating one day and most depressing the next; such are the vagaries of making crystal glass.

"I have found the people engaged in the industry are most interesting and friendly, which I find very different from a number of industries with which I was associated prior to becoming involved with glass."

In 1967, the Dennis glassworks was modernised. A new extension designed to provide more efficient flow line production on one level was built, doing away with the previously inconvenient and inefficient two floor working.

Some old buildings were demolished, the extension occupying their sites and the factory yard. Within the 25,000 square feet is a new processing room, a marking room, a cutting, intaglio and engraving department, a washing and acid polishing department, an inspection and badging room and a warehouse and despatch department.

Modern semi-automatic machinery from Belgium has been installed for "cracking-off"—the removal of surplus glass from wine glasses and tumblers and for grinding the rims. In the decorating departments, Czechoslovakian glass cutting machines with automatic wheel dressing attachment and purpose built British machinery for cutting, puntying, stoppering and intaglio replaced out-dated equipment. This modernisation has helped Webb's to maintain its pre-eminence in the production of English lead crystal glass.

During the 1950's, The Council of Industrial Design decided to keep certain specimens of Webb glass in their library as a permanent record. By 1959, they had acquired 50 designs, more than half of which were on show. In 1957, the Council awarded Webb's a certificate for the Connoisseur set of wine glasses as a product "of outstanding design."

Webb's award-winning career continues to the present time. In February 1978 the firm gained the Supreme Award sponsored by the Giftware Association and Trade Promotion Services Limited, the award being for the best article submitted in all three divisions—Home, Fashion and Originality. The occasion was the International Spring Fair held at the National Exhibition Centre in Birmingham, the first time such a competition had been arranged.

The winning exhibit was a Bristol Blue ship's decanter, designed by David Hammond, Dema's Chief Designer. Mr. Hammond trained at the Royal College of Art, London, joining Webb's in 1947. He has designed a wide range of glass-ware, including a number of commemorative pieces.

London 1884

Melbourne 1880

Sydney 1879

Paris 1889

Paris 1878

Exhibitions and awards up to 1909

Exhibitions and Awards

1851	Great Exhibition, Crystal Palace, London	Medal for cut glass
1862	International, London	
1876	Worshipful Company of Glass Sellers, Alexandra Palace, London	
1878	Paris	Grand Prix
1879	Sydney	Gold Medal for Glass
1880	Melbourne International	Gold Medal for Engraved Glassware
1884	International Health Exhibition, London	Gold Medal
1884-5	Jubilee of Victoria	Gold Medal
1885	International Inventions, London	Gold Medal for General Exhibit of Glass
1886	International Exhibition, Science and Art Edinburgh	Gold Medal for Cut and other Glass
1888	Melbourne Centennial International	First Order of Merit for Art Glass
1889	Paris	Grand Prix
1891-2	Launceston	Special First for Artistic White China and Lamp Shades of Pleated Paper
1894	Imperial Institute, London	
1908	Franco-British, White City, London	Grand Prix for Table & Ornamental Glass
1909	Imperial International, White City, London	Grand Prix for Cut, Engraved and Sculptured Glass

(The majority of the above certificates and replicas of the medals have been preserved at Dennis Glass-works).

1909
IMPERIAL INTERNATIONAL EXHIBITION,
THE GREAT WHITE CITY. SHEPHERD'S BUSH, LONDON, W.
DIPLOMA FOR GRAND PRIX.
Awarded to THOMAS WEBB & SONS LIMITED,
FOR
CUT, ENGRAVED & SCULPTURED GLASS.
Strathcona
PRESIDENT.
Imre Kiralfy
COMMISSIONER GENERAL.

Webb glass of yesterday

So far, we have dealt with the principals of the firm and events in its history. No business can survive without wise management and direction, nor can it prosper without the hard work and skills of its workers, which in a craft industry must be of a high order. Webb's have been fortunate in both respects; its distinction is due, in no small measure, to those technicians and craftsmen who produced, and often pioneered, the many types of decorative and table glass for which the firm became internationally famous.

In the following pages appears a dictionary of some of the more notable types of Webb glass. Space is limited and a great deal more research is needed, but one day it is hoped that a more comprehensive work on the Webb glass will appear.

With so many types of glass and thousands of patterns, it is but a brief selection. References are made to publications which give fuller details in some cases. Generally, a most helpful work has been Albert Christian Revi's "Nineteenth century glass," an excellent pioneer work which has a number of references to Webb glass. The present writer is most grateful to Mr. Revi for drawing attention to patents and other sources of information.

A Webb "Fish" vase was exhibited at the Imperial Institute, London during May 1894. This was glass of various colours melted together and cut, carved and pinched.

Alexandrite

Alexandrite was one of the shaded glass-wares which became popular at the end of the 19th century, being a transparent glass shading, by re-heating, from yellow to rose-red and then to blue. Corning Glass Museum, New York has a specimen as well as the Glass Collection at Stourbridge.

(Webb's Alexandrite is not to be confused with that of Stevens and Williams, Brierley Hill, the latter having a body of transparent yellow, cased with blue and rose-red, which was cut to various depths by the decorator.

Burmese

On 15th December 1885, Frederick S. Shirley patented a shaded glass-ware known as "Burmese" for the Mount Washington Glass Company, New Bedford, Massachusetts. The following year, in June, the American firm took out an English patent and shortly afterwards Thomas Wilkes Webb purchased a licence to manufacture "Burmese" in England.

As previously mentioned, there was nothing new about shaded glass-ware, but "Burmese" became the most popular. The formula comprised silica, lead oxide, pearl ash, nitre, sodium bicarbonate, fluorspar and feldspar—the "batch" for opal glass—to which was added minute quantities of uranium oxide and gold in solution. The uranium gave the opal a yellower tone. After the molten glass was gathered on the blowing-iron it was allowed to cool slightly and then was re-heated at the furnace. The portions most affected by re-heating shaded from the yellow to pink when the glass cooled.

Queen Victoria was attracted by the American "Burmese" and ordered a tea-set in this ware. Thomas Webb's was made plain, or decorated with enamel colours and gilt in varying sizes, becoming known as "Queen's Burmese," with a paper label or incised mark. Webb pattern books show a number of "Burmese" varieties, for example:

15756 (diamond mould) satin Burmese vase or tube
15757 Mat Burmese water waved vase or tube
15761 9″ vase Burmese air twist
15772 11″ vase Burmese Blue shaded water waved
15773 9″ vase Burmese Blue spiral twist
15792 6¼″ vase American Burmese

This selection dates from October and November 1886. During the following year, apart from vases, tubes and violet bowls, the firm produced all kinds of table-glass in "Burmese"—sugar and finger bowls, plates, jugs, biscuit barrels, butter dishes, marmalade jars and pickle jars.

Plain and decorated Webb's Burmese (Sotheby's)

Cameo glass

The art of carving cased glass, not practised since Roman times, was revived in the Stourbridge area during the last quarter of the 19th century, when John Northwood the First in 1876 completed his copy of the Portland Vase, the best known example of Roman cameo glass (now in the British Museum). Webb's were soon involved in the most skilful of all forms of glass decoration. The Northwood School (later at Stevens and Williams), the Lechevrel and Locke School at Richardson's and the Woodall School at Webb's gave Stourbridge glass a new importance and prestige, for nothing like it was produced elsewhere in the country. The earliest English cameo glass was hand carved. Glass of one colour, brown or blue for instance, was cased over with glass of another colour, usually opaque white ("opal"). At Webb's, George Woodall tended to use white glass with a bluish tinge which, when thinned, became rather more transparent than the denser opaque white of Northwood. Sometimes there was more than one casing, but the method of decoration was the same. The white casing was removed completely in parts to form the brown or blue background. This removal was usually done by hydrofluoric acid, although at least one cameo artist did this first stage by hand. The casing which remained was then carved or sculptured by steel chisels to create the pattern. By thinning the casing in varying degrees, the darker body colour began to show through with varying intensity, producing a three-dimensional appearance with tonal effects of light and shade. This is vividly exemplified in the drapery of classical figures.

As already mentioned, it was Thomas Wilkes Webb who encouraged his cameo artists to move from floral patterns to the portrayal of the human figure. The brothers Tom and George Woodall are the best known of Webb artists, but Kretschmann, Facer, Farmer, Davies, Smith and O'Fallon should not be overlooked. Jules Barbe, enameller and gilder, added gilt decoration to cameo pieces.
The demand for cameo glasss was such that in order to produce more pieces, the wheel began to take over from the chisel; a larger piece would be a team effort. The famous Woodall 'team' comprised Tom Hill, Tom Woodall, William Mullett, George Woodall and J. T. Fereday. Much simpler and sparser decoration, mainly floral patterns, was the feature of the cheaper "commercial" cameo. Eventually elsewhere the final indignity was the appearance of a much cheaper glass-ware, with thick white enamel painted decoration, vaguely imitating cameo, such as the popular "Mary Gregory" type.

During the 1880's, most Webb cameo glass was produced for the American market, but towards the end of the decade there was a decline in demand for cameo and ornamental glass. No doubt to counter the loss in high priced glass "novelty type" cameo was introduced. Thomas Wilkes Webb took out a patent for this in 1887, featuring "old ivory" or white opaque glass thinly cased with transparent coloured glass which was partly or wholly etched away leaving an ivory or a white background with a shaded pattern ("dolce relievo"). The old ivory effect was heightened by a brown stain.

Sometimes in this cheaper cameo the body was not wholly cased but patches of coloured glass were applied to the body and these were decorated by wheel.

Another innovation was the French style of cameo introduced by the Bohemian, Ludwig Kny.

Although the finest cameo never again became a commercial proposition, it is interesting to read that in the ninth annual meeting of shareholders held in December 1895, Charles Webb reported "that during the last few months there had been a most encouraging improvement in the demand for high-priced glass and they had recently booked orders for several expensive cameos and other decorative pieces."

Further reading:

G. W. Beard	Nineteenth century Cameo glass	Ceramic Book Co., 1956
John Northwood II	Stourbridge cameo glass	Society of Glass Technology 1949

Mr. & Mrs. Grover, of Naples, Florida, U.S.A., are currently writing a comprehensive and authorative work on cameo glass, with a large number of coloured illustrations; this should be published in America during 1980, if not before).

George Woodall cameo glass plaque c. 1885 Aphrodite D 10⅝" (Sotheby's)

Cameo vase with gilt decoration by Jules Barbe H. 11" (Private collection)

Detail from George Woodall cameo vase "Euterpe"

Cut glass

Few people nowadays realise under what conditions cut glass was made until recent years. The men who made the glass worked six hours on and six hours off, with a break at weekends. They worked in conditions which would not be tolerated today. The glass-house had no real ventilation, little light and was a place full of soot, sulphur and other fumes from coal firing. Greater credit, therefore, to the glass-makers of yesterday.

The cutters too worked in a different atmosphere. The cutting shop was a maze of wheels, belts and pulleys. In this place the hand polishing was also done, literally a lethal occupation. After the "rough" and "smoothing" cuts had been done before the days of acid polishing, the "smoothers" then got to work to restore the brilliance of the glass. Hand polishing was done by wood and cork wheels. The wood wheels, usually made of poplar, had to be continually re-shaped to fit the cuts and where there was a great amount of cutting, it took longer to polish than to cut. The wood wheels had to be fed by water and pumice (powdered by hand). The second stage was done by brush or cork wheels also fed by water and pumice. Unfortunately, the final stage of polishing was carried out by brush wheels using putty powder. This poisonous concoction consisted of lead and tin oxides. With little or no protection, the polishers quickly poisoned themselves.

Another volume would be needed to deal adequately with the thousands of Webb patterns for cut glass. With mitre-edged or rounded stone wheels were produced the diamond patterns of various types, and such popular motifs as balls, beads, gothics, splits, hollows, mirrors, flowers, rosettes, lines, fringes, flutes, pillars, scallops, jewels, stars—to mention some of those appearing in the fascinating pattern books.

The show room at Dennis Glass-works displays a wealth of cut glass, and a visit and a glance through the pattern books would give some insight into the extensive range of English lead crystal at its finest.

Nineteenth century cut designs (Webb's)

Engraved glass

For a century, since the days when Thomas Wilkes Webb brought over to this country the Bohemians—the Knys, Fritsches, Bohm and Palme—the firm has been famed for its engraved glass.

In this highly skilled decorative technique, a revolving copper wheel (from the size of a pin head to 3″ diameter) fed by oil and emery powder, delicately portrays a human or animal form, flowers, buildings, coat-of-arms and emblems with appropriate lettering. Calling for great artistic ability and craftsmanship, the engraver works with misleading ease and calm which in no way indicates the years of training and experience necessary to achieve such skill.

It should be remembered that the old engravers operated the engraving wheel by means of a treadle which they had to work with their own foot up to 100 times per minute, making their masterpieces even more creditable.

Apart from the Bohemians mentioned, the Webb pattern and price books record such names as Hockey, Hingley, Pazalt, Lewis and Dagniar (a descendent of the famous foreign glass-makers, the Dagnias who settled in the Stourbridge district in the 1670's?).

Webb engraved glass consists of ornamental and table glass and also more individual pieces to commemorate people and events. Fortunately, many of these outstanding works of art are still preserved in various parts of the world, including Webb's own showrooms.

Crystal vase with Elgin figures by F. E. Kny. H. 7½″ (Private collection)

Bowl, engraved and signed by H. J. Boam. H. 10¼" (Dudley Borough)

Etched glass

During the 1860s Webb's were producing etched glass. Towards the end of the century some was being done by outside specialist firms such as J. and J. Northwood, of Wordsley, and Guest Brothers, of Brettell Lane.

By the 1920s Webb's had set up a new etching department run by Sid Field, a talented but underrated craftsman. Field had trained at Richardson's, a pioneer firm in etching. Much of the work done towards the end of the 1920s was tableware for the Cunard Line.

During the 1930s the demand for etched glass declined, and to maintain the department "pseudo-cameo" glass was introduced. Blown in "lily" and "tulip" pattern moulds, the background was etched away by hydrofluoric acid and the whole decoration was then finished by craftsmen in the etching, intaglio and engraving departments. Pseudo-cameo was made in six colours—gold ruby, blue, amethyst, amber, green, and citron.

In simple etched glass-ware the surface was covered with an acid resist such as beeswax and resin. Two well known motifs were the circle, and Grecian key. The glass was then dipped into the acid which "ate" into the parts where the resist had been removed. The glass was then thoroughly cleaned.

Some of the last Webb etched items were commemoration pieces for Edward VIII's Coronation, designed by Tom Pitchford. Although the Coronation did not take place, these souvenirs were sold to collectors some years later.

The etching department closed towards the end of the 1930s.

Crystal vase cased with green, background acid etched. "Pseudo Cameo" H. 8" (Dudley Borough)

"Gay" glass

In the 1930's a new range of attractive glass-ware appeared. "Gay Glass" was produced in three colours—"Spring" (a delicate shade of green), "Sunshine" (golden amber) and "Evergreen," (a revival of the old "Bristol" green). These had Plain, Venetian Ripple, or Old English Bull's Eye finish, or they were cut with a water lily design. This range of different shapes and sizes, was also produced in crystal.

Gilt decoration

Gilt decoration is a centuries-old form of enhancing the beauty of glass, but a new type of gilding was introduced towards the end of the 19th century. Until then gilding had been "flat"; the innovation was "raised" gilt. Jules Barbe at Webb's and Oscar Pierre Erard at Stevens and Williams were responsible. Barbe had studied the art of gilding in France, coming to the Stourbridge district in 1879 and working exclusively for Webb's until 1900 when he became a free-lance. His home and studio were in King William Street, Amblecote.

In "raised" gilt, gold in a dissolved state was made into a brown paste, which was painted onto a glass and fired in a specially constructed muffle, two, three or four times. The gilding was finally burnished with spun glass brushes and agate or bloodstone.

The secret of Barbe's preparation died with him.

Group of Barbe enamel and gilt pieces. (Webb's)

Loving cup with gilt decoration by Jules Barbe H. 9¾″ (Dudley Borough)

Iridescent & bronze glass

In August 1877, Thomas Wilkes Webb took out a patent for a new type of iridescent glass. First exhibited at the Paris Exhibition the following year "Bronze" glass was not then on the market but shortly afterwards, in August 1878, it was on show at Goode's, South Audley Street, London. Admired by Queen Victoria, the Trade Journal described it as a glass with a surface resembling bronze of purplish tone reflecting the colours of the rainbow. In 1878 Thomas Wilkes took out another patent for iridescent glass with crackled effects.

"Bronze" glass was inspired by ancient glass which had iridised through the centuries, copying not only the appearance but also the classical shapes. Manufacture was simple but not very health-giving; in a closed muffle fumes of evaporated tin and other metallic salts were absorbed into the molten surface of the glass.

A wide range of "Bronze" was made. One of the earliest patterns (10756) was for a covered jug, then vases, candlesticks, sugars, creams, toilet sets, cruets and ice-pails are recorded. Amongst the more unusual items are a biscuit box, diamond mould (11193), etched vases (11202 etc) and gilt vases (11252 etc).

Other coloured glasses, such as peach, were also iridised.

Iris glass

This was another Thomas Wilkes Webb patent exhibited at the Paris Exhibition of 1878. "All the colours of the rainbow are reflected in this beautiful material... seen better in the shade than in light." So eulogises the Birmingham Daily Gazette of 17th April, 1878.

Patterns 10730 to 10733 are Green Iris Vases. Salt-cellars, ribbed bottles, ice-plates as well as gilded and painted decanters, were in Iris Glass.

Lemonescent

Webb's name for a type of opalescent glass known elsewhere as "straw" or "yellow" opalescent and called by modern collectors "Vaseline glass" was "Lemonescent." Using arsenic which produced the opalescence and a uranium compound, sodium diuranate or potassium diuranate which produced the colour, by re-heating the arsenic came to the surface of the glass on the parts most affected giving it a cloudy appearance, the combined effect of opalescence and colour being most attractive.

Opal

Four types of "Opal" glass were made by Webb's—a fluoride opal for ordinary lighting ware using Icelandic fluorspar (calcium fluoride) and felspar; a phosphate opal made with bone ash (calcium phosphate); arsenic opal and tin opal. These last types were used for the decorative glassware enamel painted and gilded.

Peach

Webb's Peach Glass was described in The Pottery Gazette during 1885 as "a delicate blend of colour shaded so as to resemble a peach." This was another of the shaded wares developed after the success of Burmese, changing from yellow to red. Peach was produced in America, Bohemia, and in the

Stourbridge district. The Webb pattern and price books list vases dated 16/11/85, "peach mat" (15397) and "peach iridescent" (15398) and (15399) while 15400 is the pattern number for a 7½ inch "peach bloom" vase. A variation of this colour is a "plum bloom" bowl (15411). Early in 1886, flint decoration was being applied to the peach body and peach was being blown in a diamond mould to produce a 6 inch bowl with a flint stem and "ivory" flowers. Another coloured glass to be used with peach was topaz.

"Bronze" vase. H. 11½" (Dudley Borough)

Rock crystal

Glass-makers have always tended to name their colourless or coloured glass after the natural precious or semi-precious stones which they are, in fact, imitating. "Rock crystal" glass reproduced artificially the purest of the silicate crystals which had been used for centuries in jewellery and for carving various objects. Clear glass dates from Egyptian and Roman times but this had slight colour. The Venetians produced a "crystallo" which was a great improvement, but it was left to the English glass-makers George Ravenscroft and Hawley Bishopp to invent the finest crystal glass made with lead oxide and potash. This was England's greatest contribution to glass-making ,a development which took place in 1675 and years following. Two centuries later, during the 1880's, appeared "Rock crystal" in France and England. In England, Webb's were the pioneers although this new glass was still the old lead crystal, but with a new type of decoration. This consisted of engraved decoration polished instead of being left matt as previously. Up till then engraving had tended to be separate or distinct from the cut decoration but as soon as it started to be polished, the two forms of decoration became blended together. The Bohemians, William Fritsche and Frederick Kny, were certainly engaged in "Rock crystal" work at Webb's. Early "rock crystal" was thick glass with deep cutting as its dominating feature, but gradually the engravers, perhaps for economic reasons, provided the main feature of the decoration.

One is tempted to trace the early "rock crystal" back to the deep pillar cut and moulded vessels. Parts of the claret jug made by the first Thomas Webb at The Platts in the 1840's, is faintly indicative of what was to follow.

The most famous of the early "rock crystal" pieces was the ewer decorated by Fritsche in 1886. This has cutting with sculptured effect, incorporating high quality engraving of Neptune's head and other marine motifs. The Fritsche Ewer is now in the Corning Glass Museum, New York.

In January 1896, The Pottery Gazette says "Messrs Thos. Webb and Sons Limited of the Dennis Glass Works, Stourbridge are producing some superb art work in glass which they have named Engraved Rock Crystal. We recently inspected part of a table service, the price of which was between three and four hundred pounds, the decanters being £36 and the wine glasses £2 apiece. When work of this character emanates from such a firm as Thos. Webb and Sons, it is a guarantee that it is far beyond the usual run of goods. They are now making this a speciality, the metal is cut away, showing the pattern where necessary in high relief in combination with the other portion of the engraved design. Each service is worked out by the artist, so that buyers who pay a high price, in consequence of the large amount of labour involved, are sure of getting something unique, and an article which nobody else can put upon their table. This is a feature which we know our American friends will appreciate."

Well into the twentieth century, Webb's produced "rock crystal" lines, but these were of a much lighter nature, both as regards the thinner glass and the cutting, engraving and intaglio work.

For details of the development of English "Rock Crystal" glass, 1878-1925, see the catalogue of an exhibition of this glass by Mr. Ian Wolfenden, staged at Dudley Art Gallery in 1976. For this exhibition the Dudley authority commissioned a piece of modern "rock crystal" and this was appropriately made by Webb's.

"Rock crystal" vase, possibly by William Fritsche H. 12" (Private collection on loan to Dudley Borough)

Ruby

A great deal of ruby glass was produced in the Stourbridge district during the latter half of the 19th century and the early part of the 20th. This ranged from the cheap copper ruby made by the smaller works and "cribs" (who bought ruby cullet—broken ruby glass—or ready made ruby glass lumps to colour their glass), to the fine gold ruby made by such firms as Webb's. There are tales about the owner of the works throwing gold sovereigns into the melting pot to make ruby glass, and there is no doubt that this was done sometimes perhaps as a piece of showmanship, but this would not be effective. The normal way was to dissolve the gold in aqua regia and pour this over the raw materials. Ruby glass was made both as a solid colour and for casing. Ruby wine glasses, for instance, had a thin casing of ruby on clear glass either inside or outside. A piece of thick ruby glass would look much darker and semi-opaque, and not such an attractive colour. Ruby glass made with gold is an attractive "pigeon-blood" red. It should be remembered that in gold ruby glass, the amount of gold is very small—only 0.03 to 0.05%. So this type of ruby glass is by no means valuable for the amount of gold it contains!

When an old pot in which gold ruby had been made, cracked and was removed, it was one of the "perks" of the worker to salvage the residual gold from the bottom.

Satin; Pearl satin

The Richardson firm in 1858 had patented a type of satin glass, and a similar patent taken out in America in 1881 was assigned to the Mt. Washington Glass Co. In 1886 the Company licensed Webb's to make this type. Three years later Webb's patented a process for making satin glass with cameo designs. Satin glass was made in various colours, relying basically for its effect on air trapped between layers of glass. This was achieved by blowing the body in a mould which left surface indentations and then casing the body. The cameo designs were acided from an additional casing of white glass.

Early satin glass had the normal shiny surface but later hydrofluoric acid and sand-blasting were used to produce matt surfaces.

Sidonian

Thomas Wilkes Webb, on 9th June 1876, patented a new kind of glass called "Sidonian" or "Allasantes." As the names imply, the idea was to create an impression of ancient glass. By trailing or threading a gathering of hot glass, re-heating and blowing again, the coloured threads expanded to produce what the Birmingham Daily Gazette of 11th April, 1878 describes:—

"coloured stria of groove-like appearance upon the white ground . . . producing pleasing effects."

Ruby overlay dish by William Fritsche D. 9" (Private collection)

Miscellaneous

At Dennis Hall is a wealth of Richardson and Webb pattern and price books dating from the early part of the 19th century, and catalogues of the 20th, presenting an impressive panorama of the products of the two firms for a century and a half. Apart from the extensive range of decorative and tableware, there is a long run of Richardson lighting patterns. Webb pattern numbers have now reached the total of 53,000—but one pattern number may include a number of items.

Of the various 20th century patterns may be mentioned a range of moulded patterns—ribonette, cascade, fir cone, wave, spiral and arabesque, showing what fine decorative effects can be attained by moulding and manipulation.

Webb glass today

Decanter and glasses from the "Wellington" suite (Webb's)

Webb glass today

The Ingredients

The pre-eminence of Webb glass is due to a number of important factors. Apart from the skills of the workers, highly efficient equipment and generally excellent working conditions, there are the ingredients and the way in which they are used.

The ingredients are the finest and purest available. The main constituent, *silica* (silicon dioxide) comes in the form of pure white sand, of constant particle size, imported from Belgium, as free as possible from impurities such as iron. Before the sand is mixed with the other ingredients it undergoes careful treatment to remove any foreign matter. *Red lead* (lead oxide) is mined in many parts of the world but Webb's use Australian red lead refined by a Chester firm.

Red lead makes glass very dense, increases its refractive index and imparts sparkle. *Potash* (potassium bicarbonate and potassium carbonate) like the lead, acts as a fluxing agent lowering the fusing temperature and thus reducing costs. The mixture fuses at 1350°C but silica alone would need to be heated to over 1700°C before fusion would take place.

Potassium Nitrate in small quantities makes the glass softer and more pliable, producing gases during melting, acting as an oxidising, fluxing and refining agent.

Arsenic in the form of arsenious oxide from Sweden in minute quantities also refines and assists decolourisation.

Carefully mixed in the correct proportions, the "the batch" is placed into the clay pots within the furnace. The pots are made with a high quality refractory clay from Halifax in Yorkshire.

Technical control at every stage of the making ensures a high quality "metal" free from the blemishes which beset earlier glass.

The costliest ingredient is the red lead. Webb glass contains 36% minimum, a high proportion which adds to the cost of the raw materials and also to manufacturing costs, as slower making results. But a high quality lead crystal is thus achieved.

Decanter commemorating the Silver Jubilee of HM Queen Elizabeth II, 1977. H. 15¼" (Webb's)

Glass-making

Visitors to the glass-house will notice that glass-makers work as teams with all their efforts perfectly co-ordinated. The number in each team depends on the article being made. The old fashioned "wine chair" (a team making wine glasses) comprised the footmaker who gathered the molten glass from the pot, marvered it, blew and then handed it to the servitor who made the stem and the foot of the vessel, attached a "gadget" to the foot then cracked off the glass from the blowing iron. This was then handed to the "boss" of the team—the workman—who sheared off the surplus and did any necessary shaping. A "boy" then took the glass to the lehr for annealing. Most of the work is done by rotating the glass attached to the blowing iron or the "gadget" along the two sloping arms of a wooden "chair," the design of which has not changed for centuries.

Very few wine glasses are now made by this process, which continued into the 1930's. New methods have greatly improved the symmetry of all glasses.

Impressive though the team-work is, the visitor will admire even more the individual skills. The craftsmen involved must know exactly how much to gather, must know just how and when to manipulate the glass—blowing, marvering, swinging, blocking, moulding, shaping and shearing. This knowledge is the result of many years of experience.

When the glass has been annealed to relieve the inherent stresses and strains, (otherwise these would cause the glass to "fly" (crack),) each piece is inspected to make sure it is perfect before being eventually taken to the decorator.

Cutting

The most widely used decorating technique for lead crystal glass is cutting. This is normally done by stone, carborundum or diamond impregnated wheels revolving at speeds varying from 150 to 4,000 revolutions per minute. In other words, from 800 surface feet a minute, 2,000 surface feet a minute at the roughing stage, and 5,000 surface feet a minute when diamond impregnated wheels are used. The wheels are fed by water. Diamond impregnated wheels have been used since 1937, originally intended for the first cuts, within limits these are now used for both the first and second cutting processes. Otherwise the first "roughing cuts are done within simple guide lines by decorators using carborundum wheels, then the "smoothers" go over these with synthetic or quarried stone wheels.

Webbs employ about 60 cutters.

Even after the smoothing cuts have been made, a dull surface is left and to restore the brilliance, a specialised polishing technique is used. The glass is dipped in a mixture of hydrofluoric and sulphuric acids a number of times and skill is needed to ensure that the keen edges of the cuts are retained.

Engraving

The art of engraving has already been described briefly in the previous section. The technique has changed very little. The tradition of fine Webb engraved glass has been carried on in recent years by George Pope and Cyril Kimberley.

During the last ten years a number of commemorative pieces have appeared, notably for Queen Elizabeth II's Coronation, Silver Wedding, and Silver Jubilee, and for Prince Charles's Investiture as Prince of Wales.

Goblet commemorating the Investiture of HRH Prince Charles as Prince of Wales in 1969 H. 6½"

Loving cup commemorating the marriage of HRH the Princess Anne to Captain Mark Phillips 14th November 1973. H. 7½" (Webb's)

Webb's "Bristol Blue" collection

Shops & Showrooms

Throughout much of their history Webb's have enjoyed happy relations with many agents, stores, shops, and customers throughout the world. It is impossible to list them all but the firm is both proud of and grateful for these pleasant connections.

In London showrooms were opened at 26 Hatton Gardens in 1908. In 1959 they were moved to 32/33 Hatton Gardens.

Index

**Denotes illustration*

"ART, FEAT AND MYSTERY"

SIR ROBERT MANSELL
(1573-1656)

An inspired glass monopolist

The Arms of Mansel

Mansell (or Mansfeeld as he subscribed himself in early years) was born in 1573, the fourth son of Sir Edward Mansell of Margam, Glamorganshire. He was related to Admiral Lord Howard, with whom he first went to sea and under whom he served later at Cadiz. For his part in this action young Mansell was knighted. In 1603 he became Vice-Admiral of the Narrow Seas, was later appointed Treasurer to the Royal Navy, and was finally elevated to the rank of Vice-Admiral of England. From 1601 to 1628 he represented various constituencies in Parliament.

But in 1973, the 400th anniversary of his birth and the 350th of his famous patent for glassmaking, we look at Mansell's business career in glass rather to his naval or political achievements.

In 1615 he joined Sir Edward Zouche who had obtained a patent for glass. He retired himself from the Navy, and apart from a brief recall in 1620 to settle the pirates of Algiers, devoted himself almost wholly to his business interests. He set about gaining control of the Zouche monopoly.

The granting of patents (monopolies) and their withdrawal was at the Crown's discretion. Originally the glass patent had been given to one Robson, but Zouche ("a courtier and drolling favourite of King James") "forc't it from him by these four verses" which greatly amused His Majesty:

Severn, Humber, Trent, and Thames,
And thy great Ocean and her Streames
Must putt downe Robson and his fires
Or downe goes Zouche and his desires.

Robson was, says Aubrey, "utterly undon, and came to that low degree of poverty that he swept the yard at Whitehall".

In 1623 Mansell was granted a new patent for exercising "the arte feate and misterie of melting and makeing all manner of drinking glasses broad glasses windowe glasses looking glasses, bugles bottles violls or vessels whatsoever made of glass of any fashion stuff matter or metal whatsoever with sea cole pitt coale or any other fewell whatsoever not being tymber or wood".

Mansell realised that to be successful he must have some control over his sources of fuel. He organised the coal-mining industry of the North-East for the service of his local glassmakers. He was also active in Midlands and South Wales coalfields. His control of the glass industry extended from London to Wemyss in the Kingdom of Fife, taking in such districts as Stourbridge and King's Lynn. He exploited Stourbridge and foreign clays for his glasshouse pots.

Although Mansell was no glassmaker himself he was a business man of genius and saw to it that his workmen produced glass of the right quality. No one person has had such an influence on all sides of the British glass industry. Mansell began an industrial organisation which was a major achievement in his time and even today seems not outmoded.

HWW/RET

Society of Glass Technology, Annual Dinner 1973.